?1 4

16.2

Faggot! Steel

MW01122474

A Toronto wri   it-
form 9 Theatr   es,
which he foun   as
publisher and editor of *Acanthus*, an art and literary magazine. He has
written twelve plays; also a poet, he is the author of *Powerland Minds*
(Fiddlehead 1979).

DATE DUE

SEP 1 3 2002		
FEB 0 4 2008	APR 0 1 2008	
OCT 0 2 2008	SEP 2 2 2008	

Faggot! | *Steel Kiss* and *Gulag*

by **Robin Fulford**

BLIZZARD PUBLISHING
Winnipeg • Niagara Falls

First published 1999 in Canada and the United States by
Blizzard Publishing Inc.
73 Furby Street, Winnipeg, Canada R3C 2A2.

Distributed in the United States by General Distribution Services,
4500 Witmer Industrial Estates, Niagara Falls, NY 14305-1386.

Cover design by Otium.
Printed for Blizzard Publishing in Canada by Transcontinental.

5 4 3 2 1

Blizzard Publishing gratefully acknowledges the support of
Canadian Heritage, the Manitoba Arts Council, and the Canada
Council to its publishing program.

Cataloguing in Publication Data
Fulford, Robin
    Faggot!
    ISBN 0-921368-88-7
I. Title. II. Title: Steel Kiss. III. Title: Gulag
PS8561.U883S7 1999   C812'.54   C99-920048-8
PR9199.3.F84S7 1999

To Ken and Sarah

*Many thanks to all those who helped
with the evolution of these plays.*

Steel Kiss

The first full production of *Steel Kiss*, produced by Platform 9 in association with Buddies in Bad Times Theatre, ran in October 1987 at the Poor Alex Theatre, Toronto, with the following cast:

NEIL	Jack Nicholsen
TONY	David Kinsman
JACK	Ron Jenkins
BILLY	Greg Morrison

Directed by Ken McDougall
Design by Stephan Droege
Original music by Gary Martin and David Hall
Stage Manager: Steve Lucas
Production Manager: Ken Winter

After further development at Carnegie-Mellon University, Pittsburgh, *Steel Kiss* was revived by Platform 9 in November 1991 at Buddies in Bad Times Theatre, Toronto, with the following cast:

NEIL	Andrew Akman
TONY	Derek Aasland
JACK	Michael Waller
BILLY	Fab Filippo

Directed by Ken McDougall
Design by Stephan Droege
Sound design by Jack Nicholsen
Stage Manager: Anne Driscoll
Production Manager: Steve Lucas

The first full production of *Steel Kiss* and *Gulag*, in repertoire, was a co-production by Platform 9 and Buddies in Bad Times Theatre and ran January 12 to 31, 1999, at the Buddies in Bad Times Theatre, Toronto, with the following cast:

NEIL	Shaun Benson
TONY	Gil Garratt
JACK	Jamie Robinson
BILLY	Paul Dunn

Directed by Sarah Stanley
Set and costume design by David Boechler
Lighting design by Andrea Lundy
Sound design by Richard Feren
and Steve GordonMarsh
Choregraphy by Learie McNicolls
Stage Manager: Kathryn Davies
Production Manager: Patrick Matheson

The author wishes to acknowledge the extensive help of director Ken McDougall in developing this script.

Characters

BILLY

JACK

TONY

NEIL

Production Notes

In this story, the hatred of one group is acted out upon another. The theatre is the park. The four teens, Neil, the eldest at nineteen, Jack, Tony, and Billy, the youngest at sixteen, are the main characters. The other main character is the victim, a young gay man. The four guys play the victim at various times, as they also play girls, mums, dads, cops, lawyers, teachers, et al. This society is characterized by leisure, boredom, and prejudice.

In order to facilitate the actors shifting roles, costume changes are a consideration. For instance, all the guys might wear leather or jean jackets or vests which they take off when they play the victim or other roles. A hat can work the same way.

The numerous short scenes can be bridged by blackouts and other obvious lighting changes combined with music or movement. There should be extensive use of heavy metal and rock music.

The secondary roles may be assigned somewhat differently than the text indicates to maximize each actor's abilities.

This play is loosely based upon the murder of a gay man in Toronto's High Park in the summer of 1985.

Scene One
Post Murder

(BILLY is pushed onto the stage. He stumbles, falls, and tries to regain his balance, but moves slowly as if he has been hurt. He lurches onto the garbage basket, then stumbles towards the park bench. He is in shock, but feels danger. Three others rush in and grab him as if to beat him. Instead, they hug him, all linking arms, infected by the energy of having just beaten up a faggot. The music builds. They separate, strutting around. JACK and NEIL slap hands in victory. They gather again into a group and wheel around in a line facing the audience. They watch, breathing hard.)

Scene Two
First Ghost Scene

(TONY as himself. JACK as dead victim.)

TONY: Who are you? ... What do you want? ... Who are you?!

(Death music. Victim does a death dance, falling to the floor.)

Scene Three
Preacher

(NEIL as preacher.)

NEIL: Children, listen to me. Our world is overrun with filth and pollution. It's on the street corners, it's in our parks, it's in the schoolyards where our children play. And it's coming to swallow us up. It's like that movie where this big black mass of ugly gooey filth is coming to eat us alive. You can't run and you can't hide, for the blob slithers and slides into every orifice of goodness and purity. There's only one way to stop it. You have to stand face to face with that blob and say no. Say no to the forces of evil it represents. Say no to communism, to pornography, to homosexuality. Diseased souls, say no to disease. Say no to that blob. "No, blob." Then say yes to the forces of goodness and purity.

Say yes to this beautiful green heaven, for it is here we shall
forever revel in the splendour of divine love.

Scene Four
Textbook

*(The guys are sitting around the park, ghetto blaster honking.
They are bored. TONY lobs a textbook at JACK. JACK heaves it
back. NEIL wanders, playing air guitar.)*

BILLY: Whaddaya wanna do?

(TONY throws the book again. JACK knocks it down.)

Let's do something.

(JACK flips the book back. TONY throws a high floater.)

Whaddaya wanna do?

*(JACK throws the book back, but NEIL intercepts and slams it
in the garbage basket)*

NEIL: We're goin' to the Brass Rail, Billy.

BILLY: All right.

*(NEIL kicks JACK's foot and leaves. BILLY skateboards out
after NEIL. TONY follows, turning up the ghetto blaster. JACK
is pissed. He kicks the basket then goes to join them.)*

Scene Five
Family

*(Billy's family: TV game show. NEIL as sister, JACK as father,
TONY as mother. BILLY is getting ready to go out. The others
are glued to the show.)*

TONY: Billy, Billy, don't be out too late now. Billy, do you hear me?

BILLY: Ya, Mum, I hear you.

TONY: Billy, why do you have to wear such stupid clothes? No one
else does.

BILLY: They're not stupid. I like them.

TONY: It just doesn't look normal.

BILLY: So what?

TONY: So it means you're not normal.

BILLY: So?

TONY: You never listen to me.

*(BILLY steps in front of the TV. They all move so they can still
see.)*

BILLY: Can I have my allowance?

JACK: I just gave you extra the other day.

BILLY: I'm broke. I want to go to a movie.

JACK: No way. Why don't you stay home for a change?

BILLY: For christ sake.

TONY: Billy, don't talk back to your father. He's had a hard day at work, haven't you dear? Don't be late now.

   (BILLY blocks his sister's view. She slaps him. He whispers in her ear.)

NEIL: What's a deviant, Daddy?

JACK: Never mind, Charlotte, just stay away from them.

BILLY: We got a deviant at school. Fucking queer.

JACK: Don't let me ever catch you saying that again.

BILLY: What?

JACK: What? You know what.

BILLY: No. What?

JACK: Don't you ever say "fuck" in my house again.

BILLY: Okay. Can I have my allowance?

JACK: Gave it to you.

BILLY: I need a bit more.

JACK: Get a job.

BILLY: I'll get one tomorrow.

JACK: Don't use that tone of voice with me.

BILLY: Shit.

JACK: There are rules. There are ways of doing things. You'll understand later.

BILLY: I understand now. I understand that you just want to tell me what to do and that just sucks shit.

JACK: *(Grabbing BILLY.)* Hey, big man. Big man, here. Look, Billy, next time just blow me a kiss, okay?

   (He pushes BILLY away.)

TONY: *(Watching TV.)* First pluck the mote out of thine own eye before thou throwest the stone.

JACK: What?

TONY: That's the puzzle dear. All she has to do now is buy a vowel.

   (All are engrossed in the show.)

Scene Six
Victim Monologue "A"

(JACK as a gay man.)

JACK: I guess I first realized it when I was in high school running track. I was on the relay team and couldn't keep my eyes off of Steve, who ran anchor for us. He had a great body. Anyway, one day we ran this relay for the city championship and we won. It was great. We went back to the locker room, everyone pumped up and really excited. So we start into the shower and Steve grabs me in a headlock. We're both nude, right, and he holds my face just inches from his cock. And he says something stupid like, "Bite the bag, Scottie." Well, I start to get turned on so I grab his balls and squeezed so hard he let go of me. Then I turned the shower on full cold. I nearly froze to death by the time he left. The next time we ran I skipped the shower. I guess that's where it all started.

Scene Seven
Teacher

(NEIL as teacher, others as students. They clown around.)

NEIL: Now, end of year averages were all around thirty-nine percent. Using the bell curve I brought them up the sixty where they belong. This being the last day of school and graduation of some of you, I've got some words to the wise. Now, it's been a great year. We've had our knocks but basically you've shaped up. Those of you who are going into the big bad world, just remember: believe in yourself. If you don't, then who will? Jack, take the pencils out of your nose. And for those of you who are going on to do post-secondary education, go for it. Give it your best shot. The world's out there and you need to be on top. Jack, detention room. And if you want to be on any of the teams next year, I suggest you go there now.

(JACK leaves.)

I hope you're going to be good kids this summer. Come on back and let me know how things are going. Now scat.

Scene Eight
Strip

(Strip joint. Music. NEIL becomes stripper, BILLY and TONY clap and whistle. JACK is the bouncer. Stripper does her routine of pelvic thrusts. TONY calls her over to dance for them.

She taunts them. Music stops, BILLY and TONY freeze watching. Stripper tantalizes them during her monologue.)

NEIL: Cunt. Vagina. Hole. Crack with big big tits. And you sit there and whistle and slap your horse hard, 'cause you've got all your inexperience to dream about, all those pictures, all those fantasies of clothes falling away, blowing off panties with cannons of cum … and that's sex for your young and sweaty minds.

(Music continues. Stripper dances. BILLY and TONY are animated again. The bouncer collars BILLY. BILLY does not have I.D. and is thrown out. TONY goes next.)

Scene Nine
The Guy

(NEIL as himself.)

NEIL: When I go out at night, I want to feel as though I'm flying. I want to be going a hundred and fifty clicks in a chopped Trans Am. I want to have a chick licking right down my chest, the gears shifting, the tires screaming, the G-force just taking her right down on me and I can't breathe the wind's so strong. Then I got nothing to worry about. I'm tired of the jerk-off systems, the bulls on any goddamn level tellin' me I'm shit. When I go out tonight, I'm gonna establish some things.

Scene Ten
Slapping Game

(The park. JACK and TONY are arm wrestling. NEIL and BILLY are two girls, Cheryl and Marcia, sitting on the bench.)

JACK: *(To someone.)* What the fuck are you looking at, you dick? Go feed the squirrels somewhere else.

(JACK beats TONY.)

Eat your Wheaties, man. Cheryl, got a smoke?

NEIL: Buy your own.

JACK: Stingy cunt.

(JACK and TONY play a slapping game.)

BILLY: What about you and Neil?

NEIL: He's still going out with that bitch.

BILLY: No he isn't.

NEIL: Yes he is.

BILLY: He is not.

NEIL: Don't fuck with me Marcia.

BILLY: I'm not.

NEIL: Hey guys, where's Neil?

JACK: Who wants to know?

BILLY: Tony? Tony? Tony?!

NEIL: Tony, Marcia wants to lick your pee pee.

TONY: How's your yeast infection, Cheryl?

NEIL: Fuck you.

JACK: What are you doing Saturday night, Cheryl?

NEIL: Who wants to know?

JACK: I do. I thought I'd buy you some flowers, take you out to dinner, maybe a movie. Then you could come back to my place and I'd fuck your lights out.

NEIL: If I want crabs, Jack, I'll go to the beach.

JACK: Okay, sweetheart. You're throwing away a golden opportunity. Did I ever tell you about the broad who crawled a mile to lay her teeth on my machine?

NEIL: She's probably a cripple who would have blown a dead bear.

JACK: No, she was prime territory. She knew what I had to offer.

TONY: Yeah, his dick.

NEIL: Probably need tweezers to find it.

JACK: Fuck off, Cheryl.

BILLY: But you got a cute ass, don't you Jack?

JACK: I got a great ass. A grown woman looked at my ass the wrong way and came thirteen times. No stoppin' her.

TONY: Took him a week to get her off his face.

BILLY: And you found out it was your grandmother.

JACK: Fuck off, Marcia.

BILLY: Eat shit, faggot.

JACK: Where's Neil, okay? That's all we want.

TONY: I know where he is.

NEIL: Where?

TONY: Not here.

NEIL: Oh gee, Marcia, he's not here. Gee, I thought he was. I got eyes, asshole.

TONY: He'll be back.

JACK: And we know when.

BILLY: So when?

JACK: When I get your mouth on my cock.

NEIL: Hey jerk, see that old bag. That's all you can get.

JACK: Hey, granny, get a load of this piece of ass. *(He moons.)* It's
hot, it's hairy, and it winks! I can even make it whistle. Listen.

(JACK whistles.)

NEIL: Oh my god. It's my Auntie Edna.

(NEIL and BILLY rush out.)

JACK: Oh Auntie Edna, take a look at this smiling hole.

BILLY: *Oooeee*, Auntie Edna. Cheryl says hi!

Scene Eleven
Second Ghost Scene

(JACK as himself. NEIL as dead victim.)

JACK: Who are you?

NEIL: I'm the one.

JACK: I don't know you.

NEIL: I'm the one from the park.

JACK: I don't know you, okay?

NEIL: You're one of them. I recognize you.

JACK: Bullshit! You're lying. You're fucking lying. He's dead.

NEIL: Touch me.

JACK: Get away from me.

NEIL: Just touch me.

JACK: Leave me alone.

NEIL: Look.

(Death music. Victim does the death dance to the floor.)

Scene Twelve
Victim Monologue "B"

(JACK as victim.)

JACK: I want it but I can't believe that I'm actually going to do it. I'm
sitting at home watching TV and I get this incredible urge to go.
Like I got to do it now. So I put my jacket on and I'm on the
street, on the way to the park. Lots of guys. I walk around slowly,
checking out the action. I tell myself it's crazy. Like I could be
arrested. But I'm excited because there's so much sex in the air.
I can smell it. I walk around slowly, checking out the action.

Everyone's trying to act cool, even though we all want to make contact. Anything could happen.

Scene Thirteen
Silent Cruise

(Night. Silent cruise scene in the park. Seductive music. The four, as gay cruisers, stand apart from each other, slowly turning from one to another, catching each other's glances. It is a ritual. One shows interest, the other turns away. Subtle overtures, subtle snubs. BILLY is the neophyte looking on. He avoids the man who advances on him, then watches him as he moves off to meet someone else. NEIL approaches JACK. They move off separately then meet. One kneels down and takes down the other's pants. They embrace. They have sex as the others look on.)

Scene Fourteen
Victim's Lover

(TONY as victim's lover.)

TONY: We would have met again. There was something between us, a certain attraction. We would have made plans to meet somewhere else, have dinner and talk, maybe go to the movies and hold hands, us getting to know each other, making love, fighting, dreaming together, talking all night about what we'd done with our lives and what we wanted to do. But it didn't happen that way. He died before we got to know each other. He was killed before we became real lovers. He was murdered before we really had a chance.

Scene Fifteen
Jack

(JACK as himself. Others as voices of his mother.)

BILLY: Just like him.

NEIL and BILLY: *(Together.)* You're just like him.

TONY, NEIL and BILLY: *(Together.)* You're always just like him.

JACK: Okay. Okay, Mum. You know what I mean? You keep saying that over and over again just to piss me off. You're driving me crazy.

NEIL: That's just

BILLY: the way

TONY: he would say it.

TONY, NEIL and BILLY: *(Together.)* Always telling me to shut up.

JACK: Mum, I didn't tell you to shut up. I asked you not to say that thing.

BILLY: It's my house. I'll say what I want.

JACK: Fine. I'll go out.

NEIL: You've always got an answer.

TONY, NEIL and BILLY: *(Together.)* He always had an answer.

JACK: Oh ya, and I bet I'm just like him, right? Gee, I've never heard that before in my whole life.

TONY, NEIL and BILLY: *(Together.)* Don't put words in my mouth.

JACK: Look, he's not part of our lives anymore. Just forget him.

TONY, NEIL and BILLY: *(Together.)* I can't forget him. I love him.

JACK: He never calls. He never writes. Fuck him.

TONY, NEIL and BILLY: You won't leave me, Jack, will you. You're still my boy.

JACK: I'm not a boy.

NEIL: You are.

JACK: I'm not.

TONY and NEIL: *(Together.)* You are.

JACK: I'm not.

TONY, NEIL and BILLY: *(Together.)* You are. You'll always be my boy.

JACK: Shut up about that!

TONY, NEIL and BILLY: *(Together.)* See, just like him.

JACK: I am not!

> *(JACK is leaving.)*

TONY, NEIL and BILLY: *(Together.)* Where are you going?

JACK: Out.

TONY, NEIL and BILLY: *(Together.)* Out where?

JACK: Just out.

TONY, NEIL and BILLY: *(Together.)* Are you coming back?

JACK: Yes, your little boy is coming back.

> *(JACK leaves.)*

TONY: Just

NEIL: like

BILLY: him.

Scene Sixteen
Principal and Coach

(The principal is talking to the media. The coach is walking back and forth along the sideline. TONY as principal, NEIL as coach.)

TONY: No, I can't understand it. In all the time they attended this school I saw absolutely no sign of the kind of behavior that would lead to this sort of thing. As principal, I'm sure I speak for my staff as well as myself when I say that we try to provide the best possible atmosphere for our students.

NEIL: Ready! Go! Come on. You're prancing around like a bunch of old ladies. This is football, not a social tea.

TONY: Sure they're here for an education, but I like to think that our job is not just to provide the tool for learning but to produce responsible adults.

NEIL: Come on, hustle!

TONY: I've always had an open door policy for my kids. But these boys, well, something obviously went wrong somewhere.

NEIL: I want to see a body count out there!

TONY: I think if you're looking for clues you should look to the home, because as hard as we try we can only do so much.

NEIL: Way to go, Jesse. Don't let that son of a bitch around the corner. Rip his face off! Okay, hit the showers.

Scene Seventeen
Third Ghost Scene

(BILLY as himself. TONY as dead victim.)

BILLY: I just want to go.

TONY: Then just touch me.

BILLY: Leave me alone.

TONY: I recognize you.

BILLY: It wasn't me.

TONY: You're one of them.

BILLY: Who are you?

TONY: I'm the one from the park.

BILLY: What do you want?

TONY: Look.

(Death music. Victim does the death dance to the floor.)

Scene Eighteen
Brown Stew

JACK: *(Singing.)* "Brown Stew, baby, just for you. Brown Stew, p-u. Brown Stew comin' down that canal all over you."
Hey Neil, you going to the dance?

NEIL: Yeah, I'm going with you assholes.

JACK: Your old lady going?

NEIL: Fuck off, Jack. I'm not her fucking secretary. We had a difference of opinion for your information. We're taking a break, okay? Now change the topic.

JACK: Okay. Okay.

NEIL: Anyone who shows up with her is dead meat.

JACK: Right on. Let's do some stompin'.

NEIL: When I need help from you to do my stompin', I'll pull your head out of your asshole.

JACK: But it's so nice in there.
(BILLY and TONY are having their own conversation.)

BILLY: Forget it, man. It's just cheap pussy in there anyway.

TONY: Next time, man, I'm gonna make him lick my asshole rosy clean and while he does it I'm gonna fart and blow his pinhead brain out his ear.

BILLY: That guy don't have a brain. He's strictly reptile, man.

TONY: Fuck him. I hope he gets AIDS up his nose. I hate it when people are ignorant. There was nothing wrong with being there. We were just giving you an education.

BILLY: Neil's chick dumped him, man. See that fucking face of his. He's pissed off. Just like somebody crapped in his lap.
(NEIL overhears and goes for BILLY.)
Oh shit. Neil don't ...

JACK: *(To TONY.)* Guess who's playin' at the dance?

TONY: I don't give a shit.

JACK: Brown Stew, man. *(Singing.)* "Brown Stew, just for you. Brown Stew, p-u. Brown Stew comin' down that canal all over you."

NEIL: *(Finished with BILLY, singing with JACK.)* "She said give me some more, right here on the floor. She said, Brown Stew, I really love you."

TONY: Sounds like something Mr. Stevens will like. He's full of shit.

BILLY: Stevens, man, he's such a fucking turd. In math class Janie sits behind me and takes off her earrings and puts them on my ears and Stevie turns and sees and is just bustin' to give me shit, but knows I'll tell him to suck it if he acts up, so he goes to put up the next math shit and steps right in the fuckin' garbage can. He's gotta be the worst.

JACK: Stevie's gonna bring his fat bag of a wife to the dance. I'm gonna ask her to dance so I get some personal experience with circumference.

BILLY: Math gives me a real hard-on.

NEIL: Fuck.

BILLY: One rod plus two nuts equals one monstrous cock, able to leap tall buildings at a single orgasm, will make Lois or any other of those sluts cream on first view. *(The others look at him like he's an asshole.)* … Ah, ya.

TONY: How do you know when your chick's too fat?

JACK: You just can't get close enough to stick it in.

TONY: When she sits on your face you can't hear the stereo.

BILLY: Well turn it up to ten and blow her off.

JACK: You know what Mouth said to me just the other day? He said I couldn't make any of the teams unless I quit smoking. Well fuck him. I was MVP the last two fucking years.

NEIL: You couldn't outrun a one-legged bitch with lung cancer, you wanker.

JACK: Is that right, you fuckwad?

NEIL: Ya, that's right.

> *(They push each other.)*

TONY: Mouth has an eye for that new broad gym teacher.

JACK: Can you see those two going at it in the gym?

BILLY: *Ooo*ahhhh. Fuck me on the parallel bars. Stick it in on the tramp. *Oooo*ahhhh. Fuck me till I come all over the pummel horse.

> *(Laughter turns to silence. They are waiting, watching.)*

JACK: Pointing. Hey, ten to one that guy's a faggot.

> *(They line up, their anger giving way to an expression of loss.)*

NEIL: It was an accident.

BILLY: We were drinking.

JACK: Things got out of hand.

TONY: We really didn't mean to hurt him.

NEIL: It was an accident.

BILLY: We were drinking.

JACK: Things got out of hand.

TONY: We really didn't mean to hurt him.

Scene Nineteen
Dad

(TONY with ghetto blaster. He is looking for his father. He keeps yelling out, "Dad." Finally he sits down on the bench and turns up the music, mouthing the words to the song. He calls "Dad" once more.)

Scene Twenty
Victim Monologue "C"

(BILLY as victim.)

BILLY: When I dream at night it goes like this. A man whose face I can't see stands before me. He undoes his pants. We both wait. He lets them down. It's my turn. But I can't move. He undoes my belt. I want to reach out and touch him. His hands slide my pants down. We are there together looking at each other in the dark. But his face is still hidden. I want to touch him. I struggle to reach out to move, but I begin to fall forward. He catches me. I look up and he's gone.

Scene Twenty-one
Love Cruise

(Night: the park. BILLY as victim and NEIL as lover.)

NEIL: Hi.

BILLY: Hi.

NEIL: Have you got the time?

BILLY: I don't have a watch. But it was ten-thirty when I left. But that was a while ago.

NEIL: Oh, good. Mind if I sit down?

BILLY: Sure … Helluva night.

NEIL: Yeah.

BILLY: Sure are a lot of people around here.

NEIL: Well, it's Friday night.

(NEIL caresses BILLY. BILLY moves away.)

What's the matter? It's dark. No one can see you except me.

BILLY: Do you come here often?

NEIL: I've seen you before.

BILLY: No, I don't think so.

NEIL: What's your name?

BILLY: I gotta go.

NEIL: Right now? We're alone. Make up a name if you want.

BILLY: What's yours?

NEIL: What would you like to call me?

BILLY: I don't know.

NEIL: Let's just sit here. I won't do anything if you don't want.

BILLY: No, I'm fine.

NEIL: Then come on, sit.

(BILLY sits.)

BILLY: You know this place well?

NEIL: Somewhat, ya. You?

BILLY: Just parts.

NEIL: It's a nice park. I like it here. I have seen you here before.

BILLY: I've been here, but I've only watched.

NEIL: Why did you come here tonight? Not just to watch?

BILLY: No.

NEIL: To talk?

BILLY: Yes.

NEIL: And what else? To fuck?

BILLY: I don't know. But I want to do something.

NEIL: All right. I like you.

(NEIL kisses BILLY's hand. BILLY pulls away.)

BILLY: What about you?

NEIL: Me?

BILLY: Why are you … why here?

NEIL: Because it's anonymous.

BILLY: What about when you meet someone you like?

NEIL: Like you? I don't come here to have a relationship. I'm married.

BILLY: What?

NEIL: That's why I come here.

BILLY: I don't understand.

NEIL: Does it matter?

BILLY: It's strange, that's all.

NEIL: Get over it.

(*NEIL kisses BILLY's neck*)

BILLY: Do you ever get scared out here?

NEIL: There's nothing to be scared of.

BILLY: I don't mean scared of you. Just scared.

NEIL: Just relax. Let go of it. Everything's gonna be just fine.

(*NEIL kisses BILLY.*)

Scene Twenty-two
Bigot

(*JACK as bigot.*)

JACK: As long as they stay out of my way they can do what they
   want, but don't tell me that what's going on with them is love.
   Love is a natural expression between a man and a woman. You
   don't cruise in the park if you're looking for love. It's only sex.
   They're not lonely, they're horny. Pure and simple. And you
   know what they're now saying about AIDS? The whole fucking
   world's gonna be infected. The faggots have spread it all around,
   right? We should do what they do in Mexico. Shave 'em bald and
   give 'em twenty-four hours to get out of town. Nazis could even
   do it better, right?

Scene Twenty-three
Drag Queen

(*TONY as drag queen.*)

TONY: Personally, I'm sick to death of the whole thing. This is the
   kind of thing that gets blown out of proportion. Who knows
   even why they did it. Maybe they were just in the wrong place at
   the wrong time. The guy who died was. I'm not being cold-
   hearted. That's the type of world we live in.

Scene Twenty-four
Wedgie Time

(*Loud music on the ghetto blaster. The guys are hacking around.
NEIL challenges TONY to a hand wrestle. He beats him.*)

NEIL: Hey Billy, high five.

(*They do high five, then NEIL bends his hand throwing BILLY*) *quickly to the ground. NEIL then challenges JACK. The match is more even. The others root for JACK, but NEIL finally beats him.)*

JACK: *(To TONY and NEIL.)* Hey boys, it's wedgie time.

(They grab BILLY, hooting and hollering.)

NEIL: Billy-boy, you're gonna be pullin' gotch outta your hole for a week.

JACK, TONY and NEIL: *(Together.)* One, two, three, *go!!*

BILLY: *(Wedgied.)* Let go! You're killing me! Fucker!

JACK: Say pretty please, faggot.

BILLY: Pretty please, faggot!

JACK: Who you callin' faggot, you little gearbox?

(They let BILLY down. TONY sees a girl.)

TONY: Well, will you looky there.

BILLY: *(To the guys.)* Bastards!

JACK: Ooooeeee, cutie. Right over here. I think she deserves me.

BILLY: Then she needs a seeing-eye dog.

JACK: Hey, free poke over here, you blessed Canadian beaver, you ultimate pelt of love.

NEIL: She's a dog. She's probably still in a training bra.

JACK: You're giving me a hard-on, man.

NEIL: Where are the women? And I don't mean that fuckin' snot-nose kid. I'm talkin' about real seasoned cunt. I mean, we got the best pud in town just sitting here like limp shit. That's not fucking right. I'm gonna be into menopause if I stand around here much longer. And when they come to get what they deserve they better have some money, 'cause I need some gas in the truck.

JACK: I bet you do.

(JACK and NEIL do a complicated jock handshake-grunting ritual. TONY becomes a girl sitting on the bench. NEIL sees her.)

NEIL: Boys, I want you to take a good long whiff. You smell that, Billy-boy. Now that's real live pussy.

(They gather around her.)

Hi. My name is Neil. So why don't you?

(The guys laugh.)

Come on, what's your name?

TONY: Suck shit.

NEIL: Is that Miss or Mrs. Shit? Come on. Let's have some fun. I can go for a week straight and come every hour on the hour.

TONY: Bet you need Novocain just to keep it up.

(She walks off.)

NEIL: Fuck you! What the hell do you know? You're nothin' but a frigid bitch. Cunt! Who gave her the right to talk to me that way? Fuck you!

JACK: I'd love to, Novocain or no Novocain. If I ever sprayed that stuff on my knob I'd be hard for a month. I love ya, baby!

BILLY: I love your ass more than my own, more than Mum's, more than Rover's.

(Pause.)

TONY: Come on, man, let's get some brewskies.

BILLY: It's Miller time.

NEIL: Ya, with what?

TONY: With all your money you should be treatin' us.

NEIL: Fuck off.

TONY: Hell, you goin' straight on us? In school you were always tanked up. You should try it again. Makes life more realistic, right?

NEIL: Times are dry, man. I'm all out. Got twenty bucks to my name. That fuckin' truck just sucks it all up.

JACK: Twenty is just enough to get the rest of the box. *(JACK pulls out a few bills.)* Come on, man. I'm thirsty.

NEIL: Get a job, man.

BILLY: Let's get some tall boys and we'll shotgun 'em.

NEIL: None of you suckers is old enough to drink. You're dickin' minors. You're nothin' but shit. You're asking me to part with my hard-earned coin. I should be heading to downtown to lay my pecker in the chops of some hooker.

JACK: Come on, man. We know you'd rather jerk off.

NEIL: Listen, asshole, you talk like that you're gonna die. Know what I mean, ass-wipe?

JACK: Kidding, kidding, man. All right?

(They start pushing each other.)

NEIL: That's for being a prick. You're nothing but a dick lick.

JACK: Don't you fucking hit me, man.

NEIL: Don't be an asshole, okay.

JACK: Okay, just don't hit.

NEIL: Or what?

JACK: Or this.

> *(JACK grabs NEIL around the knees and throws him up onto his shoulders. He jumps up and down bouncing NEIL's groin into his shoulder.)*

NEIL: Ahhh! You're killing me!

JACK: You gonna do it again?

NEIL: Ahhh!

JACK: Eh?

NEIL: Don't!

JACK: You want pancakes for nuts? Eh?

NEIL: Jesus!

> *(JACK whirls NEIL around and around.)*
>
> *Fuuuck!!*

Scene Twenty-five
Fourth Ghost Scene

> *(NEIL as himself. BILLY as dead victim.)*

NEIL: It wasn't me, okay?

BILLY: That's not true. You took three kicks. The first one got me in the head. The other two in the stomach.

NEIL: You've got no proof of that.

BILLY: I was there.

NEIL: So was I. How come I don't remember it that way?

BILLY: Touch me.

NEIL: Fuck you. You're not a real person.

BILLY: It was your idea.

NEIL: It was no one's idea. We just did it before and everything turned out all right.

> *(Victim leaves.)*

Hey, come here. You wanna kick me in the balls? You want your revenge? Well come and do it … Please!

Scene Twenty-six
Girlfriend

(NEIL swinging a baseball bat. Everytime he swings the others make a slapping sound that echoes. They play Neil's girlfriend.)

TONY, BILLY and JACK: *(Together.)* Neil … Neil … Neil?

TONY: Why won't you talk with me?

BILLY: I miss you.

JACK: I just want to talk to you.

TONY: I just want to be friends.

NEIL: Shut up!

> *(Swing, slap.)*

TONY, BILLY and JACK: *(Together.)* Neil … Neil … Neil?

TONY: I couldn't go out

BILLY: with you

JACK: anymore.

> *(The sequence "I couldn't go out / with you / anymore" is repeated three times.)*

NEIL: Shut up!

> *(Swing, slap.)*

TONY: You shouldn't have hit me.

BILLY: You shouldn't have hit me.

JACK: You shouldn't have hit me.

NEIL: I didn't want to.

TONY: You shouldn't have hit me.

NEIL: I didn't want to.

BILLY: You shouldn't have hit me.

NEIL: You said those things and my hand came up.

JACK: You shouldn't have hit me.

NEIL: You bitch! *(Swing, slap.)* You fucking bitch! *(Swing, slap.)* You bitch! *(Swing, slap.)* Bitch! Bitch!

> *(The others close in on him. Swinging, slapping.)*

Scene Twenty-seven
Keep 'Em Out

(The park.)

BILLY: Keep 'em out of our park.

JACK: Fuckin' queers.

NEIL: They're all over the place.

JACK: Why the fuck are they allowed to do that shit?

TONY: Get the pigs on their ass. This is a public place.

JACK: They don't give a shit about that. They pay the cops off.

BILLY: You have to be a faggot to be a cop.

NEIL: Oh suck off, man.

TONY: Fuck, man, they make me wanna puke.

NEIL: Fuckin' pecker, fuckin' cocksucker.

BILLY: We need us a dozen eggs.

JACK: On Hallow-fucking-we'en, man, I know where we go with the eggs this year.

BILLY: Let's go tell one of those bastards what we think of them. They need to be talked to. Fuck 'em.

JACK: You're all talk, Billy-boy.

>   *(Pause.)*

NEIL: Hey, he one of them? Hey you, come here. Come on I want to talk to you.

JACK: Ya. Just prances along. See, he's chicken shit. Saw us, now he's going the other way. Hey, asslick!

NEIL: Hey, you!

JACK: Fuckin' blow boy. You wanna date with me? Well, dream on, buddy.

>   *(They are waiting, bored.)*

TONY: Okay, I got three bucks for beer.

NEIL: Hell, I wouldn't let you give me head for that.

TONY: Come on, I thought you guys were thirsty.

JACK: Look at the refu-fucking-gees. Hey, towel head, hey, go back where you come from. We don't need your shit sneaking into this country. Fuck I hate Pakis.

NEIL: Niggers, man.

BILLY: Kikes.

JACK: They're all over the fucking place. And they stink, man. They just fucking stink. Hey, buddy, hey, why don't you use some Ban. Hey, use some Right Guard, you fucker. *(Sprays on deodorant.)*

NEIL and BILLY: *(Together—paddling a boat; Indian accent.)* Run away and go to Canada. Going to Canada. Open convenience store. Land! Land! Canada! Canada!

TONY: This is boring, man.

JACK: So make something happen.

TONY: I'm just fucking thirsty, okay?

JACK: So make it, man.

NEIL: Okay, okay. If you can tell me what the most provocative thing a broad can wear behind her ears, I'll buy the rest of the case.

BILLY: What's provocative?

NEIL: It means your dick wants to do pushups. Don't worry, when you get your first hard-on you'll know what I mean.

BILLY: Eat me.

TONY: Perfume, that's what she wears.

NEIL: Nope.

JACK: Beer.

NEIL: Nope.

TONY: Pizza with anchovies.

BILLY: Your dirty underwear. Your mother's dirty underwear.

TONY: Fuck, this better be good.

NEIL: Hey man, the most provocative thing a broad can wear behind her ears is her ankles, her fucking ankles.

(They don't get it.)

Her fucking ankles, man.

(NEIL gets down and tries to put his feet behind his ears. He pretends he is a girl getting it, ooo's and ahhh's.)

JACK: Oh fuck off.

BILLY: Ankle a bit of this.

(BILLY grabs NEIL's spread legs and rubs his groin with his foot. Death music. BILLY throws NEIL's legs away. NEIL becomes the victim lying on the ground. BILLY, TONY and JACK punch and kick him.)

Scene Twenty-eight
Interrogation

(This scene shifts back and forth between the police interrogation and immediately after the murder.)

TONY: *(As cop.)* What happened?

NEIL: I don't know.

BILLY: *(As cop.)* Tell us.

NEIL: It just happened.

JACK: *(As cop.)* How did you feel?

NEIL: They're faggots.

TONY: *(As cop.)* You hated them?

NEIL: They're queers.

***

BILLY: What are we gonna do now?

JACK: Let's party.

TONY: He's bleeding.

NEIL: Everybody bleeds, man. Come on, let's go.

BILLY: He's just lying there.

JACK: Forget it, man. Let's go. I need a drink.

***

TONY: *(As cop.)* What does "queer" mean?

JACK: Look, I can't figure them out. That night, it was like things weren't real. Just leave me alone.

NEIL: *(As cop.)* As soon as I understand.

JACK: We're not to blame.

BILLY: *(As cop.)* Then who is?

JACK: If they weren't hanging around our park then it wouldn't have happened.

***

TONY: Let's get out of here.

BILLY: We just gonna leave him?

JACK: He's a faggot. He knew what to expect.

NEIL: We were just having some fun.

TONY: Fuck, look at that blood.

***

JACK: *(As cop.)* Tell us.

BILLY: We were walking in the park. We'd drunk too much. Then there was this guy there.

NEIL: *(As cop.)* Did he do anything to you?

BILLY: He was there. That was enough. He was there and he was a faggot. Why don't you understand that?

TONY: *(As cop.)* What did he do to you?

BILLY: We saw him and … then I don't know.

TONY: *(As cop.)* What happened?

***

BILLY: You really smashed him, man.

JACK: Fuckin' right.

TONY: I mean, it's like the movies.

NEIL: Like taking down some fucking gook or something.

JACK: Just did him in.

***

TONY: *(As cop.)* What happened?

NEIL: He was there.

TONY: *(As cop.)* What did you say to him?

NEIL: Faggot!

JACK: Cocksucker!

BILLY: Assfuck!

TONY: *(As cop.)* What happened?

NEIL: It was dark.

JACK: *(As cop.)* What happened?

NEIL: He tried to run.

BILLY: *(As cop.)* What happened?

Scene Twenty-nine
Victim Monologue "D"

(NEIL as victim.)

NEIL: What really happened was that things were different. Different inside. I was different than the others. I felt things they could never understand, so I could never tell them or anyone. I had these feelings about … about other guys and I kept being afraid because that's supposed to be wrong, but I didn't know why. If you don't fit in, then you're dead. Even if you do fit in you aren't safe for long. You try to be one thing and you're really another and then you're caught.

TONY: What happened?

NEIL: It was an accident.

BILLY: We were drinking.

JACK: Things got out of hand.

TONY: We didn't really mean to hurt him.

Scene Thirty
The Car

(The park. The guys are drinking.)

JACK: Fuck off, Billy.

NEIL: You gotta understand that the car has to fit the driver, like an extension of his personality. Ya know what I mean?

BILLY: Give me a '56 Chevy souped up to go and I'm tellin' you I'll never be the same.

TONY: Hey man, you deserve a Honda Civic.

JACK: Billy-boy, you don't even have your license. You're a little puke.

BILLY: Don't matter. This is what you do. You got the brake on and you keep goosin' her, letting out the clutch till she catches, spinnin' the back tires so they heat up. When they're ready to stick like glue you pop her and go crazy.

NEIL: You don't understand what I'm sayin', man. I'll put it in simpler terms. There are a number of conditions a car has to fit. The first is that you gotta be able to fuck in it. But that doesn't mean nothin'. Hell, even if you have an MG all you gotta do is open both doors. So if you got the parts you can do it in any car, right? The second thing is that you gotta have noise. You don't have the blast comin' out the ass then you are nowhere, no matter how fast you go. The third thing you need is balls under the hood, big mother-fucking balls. When I see a chopped Trans Am, I just know it deserves my ass. Like it's a feeling. I gotta get rich fast. Jesus.

TONY: You got the wheels, you got the pussy.

BILLY: Pull right up to some Spandex mama and say, hey baby, just slide your tight twat in. And if you got the machine she's gonna say …

JACK: Eat me right here on the hood.

TONY: Stick it in on the trunk.

> *(Laughing, pause.)*

NEIL: So what's gonna happen tonight. We just gonna sit here getting pissed?

JACK: What's the matter with that, man?

NEIL: Nothing's the matter with it, but it's not enough, now is it?

Scene Thirty-one
Doctor

(They are more drunk.)

JACK: How come there gotta be faggots anyway? I mean, what the fuck is their game.

BILLY: Up the ass.

NEIL: They're sick, man.

JACK: My fuckin' doctor wanted to shove his finger up my ass. I told him to eat shit and do it fast.

NEIL: Fist fuckin', man. Bend over, cutie, here comes my bullet.

JACK: I just go in for a regular check-up, you know, and he says now bend over, and he puts on this glove like he's about to get a hard-on.

TONY: You'd probably do it yourself if you had the coordination.

JACK: Suck shit, man. I don't have OHIP [Blue Cross] so those assholes can get their rocks off. We should put all the faggots and all the doctors in one room and shoot the whole fucking shebang. That oughtta give us some breathing room, right?

NEIL: Gimme a beer, man.

JACK: Oh, so you want a beer?

> *(JACK pours beer in NEIL's mouth. NEIL spits it out at JACK.)*

Scene Thirty-two
Beer Can

(The guys are sitting on a park bench. They are silent and dangerous. The wait seems endless. Then BILLY crunches up a beer can and throws it at the garbage basket.)

Scene Thirty-three
Attack

(JACK is lookout. The others are hidden.)

BILLY: So we gonna do it or what?

JACK: *(Sitting on bench.)* Ya, man, ya ... Fuck, here comes one.

NEIL: Don't get excited.

BILLY: Let's go smooth and quiet.

TONY: Like nothin's gonna happen.

JACK: Here he comes.

BILLY: We got a surprise for you, faggot.

NEIL: Shut up, Billy.

JACK: Come on, man. Let's get him.

TONY: He ain't goin' nowhere.

NEIL: He won't know what hit him.

TONY: Let's put the cocksucker away.

NEIL: Act like a faggot, man.

JACK: Here he comes. First blood, man. First fucking blood.

NEIL: This is gonna be better than an orgasm.

JACK: Fuckin' lay him out.

BILLY: Now!

(They rush forward.)

Scene Thirty-four
The Autopsy

(NEIL does the death dance.)

TONY: External marks of violence:

JACK: multiple bruises on forehead

BILLY: corner of right eye

JACK: bridge of nose

BILLY: left side of cheek and on lips

JACK: abrasions on left leg, back, and right elbow

TONY: all of recent origin

JACK: left ear bruised and swollen with lacerations.

TONY: Scalp:

BILLY: multiple hematomas on right and left sides.

TONY: Skull:

JACK: fracture of left occipital bone.

TONY: Brain:

BILLY: showed a diffuse subarachnoid hemmorrage

JACK: was soft and swollen

BILLY: bruise marks behind right ear.

TONY: Cause of death:

JACK: severe cranio-cerebral injuries.

Scene Thirty-five
Courtroom

TONY: When I was arrested, my parents went totally crazy. They just sat there and cried. I couldn't say nothin'. I stood between two cops. They told them. I felt sick, man. Went upstairs and puked, all grey and green, like my insides were rotten. I had to force myself so I didn't think of that guy. I mean, it was all wrong. I couldn't believe he was dead.

JACK: *(As cop.)* Yes, Your Honour, this kind of thing happens all the time. Usually when kids like this are involved it rarely goes beyond a common assault. And we know that that kind of assault happens far more frequently than is actually reported to us. It's like women and rape. A lot of gay victims, and witnesses for that matter, do not want to stand up in court. It's the old fear thing. If the victim in this case hadn't died as a result of the beating, it probably would have gone unreported …

NEIL: *(Court Official.)* All rise.

BILLY: *(Court Official.)* How do you plead?

NEIL: Guilty.

BILLY: Guilty.

JACK: Guilty.

TONY: Guilty.

BILLY: To the lesser charge of manslaughter.

NEIL: *(As victim's father.)* It was my son they killed. It was murder. You can't change the word. They killed him for no other reason than that he was different from them. I want those bastards to pay for what they did to my boy.

TONY: *(As defendant's father.)* My boy's not a bad boy. He's got to pay for what he did. But you gotta understand that he's not a hardened criminal. You put him in jail now and you throw out every chance he has. If he was your boy you'd feel the same way.

He'd never do anything like that again. I think he's innocent. He just made a mistake.

NEIL: *(Court Official.)* Approach the bench.

TONY: *(Judge.)* I sentence you to five years in the federal penitentiary.

NEIL: It was an accident.

BILLY: We were drinking.

JACK: Things got out of hand.

TONY: We didn't really mean to hurt him.

NEIL: *(As they cover their faces from the cameras.)* We'll be out in two.

Scene Thirty-six
Victim Monologue "E"

(NEIL and BILLY, as two gay men, lie on the ground beginning to make love. JACK, as JACK, sits on the bench. TONY as victim.)

TONY: In the dark, in the shadow, I touch someone. I walk into arms that squeeze me hard. We press against each other. I open my mouth and kiss him. He pulls me down, his hands under me, taking me. There's nothing else in the world but the two of us. All I know is how I feel and I don't want it to change, ever. His eyes are like black diamonds on this night. I love him and he loves me. It has to be that way.

(JACK invades the victim's space. He stares dangerously. Freeze.)

Gulag

Gulag was developed by Platform 9 Theatre and first produced by Platform 9 and Theatre Passe Muraille, Toronto, running September 26 to October 20, 1996, with the following cast:

NEIL	Jason Cadieux
TONY	Balazs Koos
JACK	Michael McMurtry
BILLY	Sam Nulf
MAN (multiple)	Michael Healey
WOMAN (multiple)	Diane Flacks

Directed by Sarah Stanley
Set design by Steve Lucas
Lighting design by Andrea Lundy
Costume design by Minda Johnson
Sound design by Richard Feren
Fight choreography by Viv Moore
Assistant Director: Franco Boni
Stage Manager: Kathryn Davies
Production Manager: T. J. Shamata

The present text of *Gulag* is a further development that was workshopped at Buddies in Bad Times Theatre's Ante Chamber Series and first produced by Platform 9 and Buddies in Bad Times Theatre. It ran in repertoire with *Steel Kiss* January 12 to 31, 1999, at Buddies in Bad Times Theatre, Toronto, with the following cast:

NEIL	Shaun Benson
TONY	Gil Garratt
JACK	Jamie Robinson
BILLY	Paul Dunn
WOMAN (multiple)	Stephanie Jones

Directed by Sarah Stanley
Set and costume design by David Boechler
Lighting design by Andrea Lundy
Sound design by Richard Feren
and Steve GordonMarsh
Choregraphy by Learie McNicolls
Assistant Director: David Duclos
Stage Manager: Kathryn Davies
Production Manager: Patrick Matheson

The author wishes to acknowledge the extensive help of director Sarah Stanley in developing this script.

Characters

BILLY
JACK
NEIL
TONY

Friends, murderers; they are
all in their early twenties.

CHERYL, Jack's girlfriend
DOROTHY, Neil's date
Billy's MOTHER
FRANIE, Tony's sister

All are played by one actress.

Setting

The play begins in the prison, moves to the outside, and concludes
at Neil's apartment. Obvious from the beginning is the costume of
Contessa, the prison drag queen, a blond wig and blue sequinned
dress.

Scene One
Manslaughter

(The park: flashback to the original murder.)

NEIL: This is gonna be better than an orgasm.

BILLY: Faggot.

JACK: Don't get excited.

TONY: That shouldn't be too hard.

(They laugh.)

BILLY: I got a surprise for you, faggot.

NEIL: Shut up, Billy.

JACK: Come on, man.

TONY: You call that a man.

(They laugh again.)

BILLY: Act like a faggot, man.

NEIL: Stop it, Billy.

BILLY: Faggot needs a kiss.

JACK: Fuckin' lay him out.

BILLY: Now!

Scene Two
Guilty

(From their murder trial. The accused line up; others are voice-overs. They take their clothes off to go to prison.)

CLERK: *(Voice-over.)* Order in the court. All rise.

JUDGE: *(Voice-over.)* How do you plead?

TONY: Guilty.

JACK: Guilty.

NEIL: Guilty.

BILLY: Guilty.

JUDGE: *(Voice-over.)* I sentence you to …

43

TONY: Here we go.

JACK: We were drinking.

BILLY: I really didn't mean to hurt him.

NEIL: You don't understand.

JUDGE: *(Voice-over.)* Approach the bench. I sentence you to the lesser charge of manslaughter.

JACK: Put us in jail now, and ...

TONY: ... we'll get out ...

BILLY: ... and then ...

NEIL: ... what are you gonna do?

Scene Three
The Hounds of Rage

(The prison shower. The guys are snapping towels at each other, cycling faster and faster. BILLY gets pinned by NEIL, the others disappearing. NEIL starts to fuck him. BILLY pulls off. NEIL leaves. BILLY approaches the Contessa costume.)

CONTESSA: *(Voice-over.)* Hey, fag killer.

BILLY: Hey, Contessa.

Scene Four
Neil's Confession

(Jail.)

NEIL: You wanna know the truth so I'm gonna tell you. My first fight, right? Lost. My second fight, lost. Then hooked up with the guys and won, won, won. And we would have won that last one too if that guy hadn't been such a faggot. I had to get it up to a certain level in order to protect myself. Because if you don't protect yourself, then you're nowhere. It's like you have to be an extension of yourself, if you know what I mean. Man, it's hot in here. It's like a pressure cooker. Don't get me wrong. I know we shouldn't have killed anybody, but I still have a hard time seeing them—homosexuals, I mean—as people. I guess maybe that's gotta change.

Scene Five
Motherlode

(Jail yard. JACK runs to BILLY.)

JACK: The motherlode, Billy-boy, the fucking motherlode has come in.

BILLY: Parole?

JACK: The mandatory four done on the twentieth.

BILLY: Hey, shit man, fuckin' freedom.

JACK: The brothers are ready once again to ride off into the sunset smelling like horseshit.

BILLY: Seen Neil and Tony?

JACK: Oh man, they'll freak. We got it, baby.

　　　(Whooping it up.)

BILLY: Jesus, man, there's still the hearing.

JACK: Don't go paranoid pussy on me, you meatball.

BILLY: But we gotta prepare.

JACK: Ya, okay. We got our Correctional Plan, Billy-boy. More or less stayed out of trouble.

BILLY: Pardon?

JACK: More or less stayed out of trouble, *sir!!*

BILLY: The fights will fuck us around.

JACK: Self-protection, your honour. I didn't want to do it.

BILLY: Jeez, man, you're good.

JACK: Think I'm good enough to get Cheryl to put me up?

BILLY: Cheryl?

JACK: I can't live with the dickweed my mom married. I'd be telling him to bite scrot morning, noon and night.

BILLY: When's the last time you talked to Cheryl?

JACK: I wrote her.

BILLY: She write back?

JACK: Not really.

BILLY: Gonna phone her?

JACK: Yep.

BILLY: Cool. Least you got a plan.

　　　(NEIL and TONY join them.)

NEIL: Plan? I got a plan.

ALL: *(Together.)* Parole! Fucking parole!

　　　(They all do a grunting, celebrating routine. NEIL jumps on BILLY.)

NEIL: Not pickin' on you, lover boy. Just celebrating freedom. Now

I've got to make it simple for you fuck-ups. And you are all fuck-ups. Anybody disagree with me? 'Cause if you think you're gonna go out into our society and spread your ex-con disease around, well, you've got another thing coming.

BILLY: Okay, Neil, are you having fun? Get off me. You smell.

NEIL: Smell! What? I don't smell. I've never smelled in my life, you germy little mother-fucker. I do not smell!

JACK: Neil? Neil?

NEIL: What?

JACK: Got that smoke?

NEIL: No.

JACK: Come on. I know you got one.

NEIL: Only one left. It's for me.

JACK: But you owe me one.

NEIL: It's my last smoke. Don't be such a prick.

JACK: You owe me the smoke, numb-nuts.

BILLY: Neil, give him the smoke.

(*NEIL gives him the smoke.*)

JACK: Thanks, Neil.

NEIL: (*To BILLY.*) Someone's gonna kick your fucking head in some day.

(*Others pretend to be scared.*)

Scene Six
Billy's Confession

(*Jail.*)

BILLY: I remember Contessa's last night. I smelled death in his drum. He looked so small there in the bed. When I tried to say goodbye he suddenly opened his eyes and tried to smile but couldn't. His lipstick was all smeared. Looked like blood. He kept trying to say something. Finally he said he loved me. And then I left. And you know what, I couldn't say it back. I wanted to, I really really wanted to say it back, but I couldn't. Because I … because I'm not a fag.

Scene Seven
Hoolas

(*TONY wakes up from a nightmare.*)

TONY: Jesus, man, I had that fucking dream again.

NEIL: Tony, that faggot died. It's time to move on.

TONY: Every time I dream of it I want to puke.

NEIL: Hey, hey, hey, man, dream about this. And I'm sayin' it for the last time. When we get out of here, we're gonna find you one great mother of a babe who's got knockers long enough to wrap around your head. And I just know that deep down inside you, what you want most of all is to bury your head between those gigantic hoolas. Now am I right or am I right?

TONY: Ya, that would be nice.

NEIL: *(As babe.)* "Come here, bad boy."

TONY: Fuckin' hoolas, man.

NEIL: "Just come lick my beautiful hoolas."

JACK: Tits 'n pussy.

NEIL: "Fur of love. Fur of love."

JACK and NEIL: *(Together.)* "Fur of love! Fur of love!"

TONY: Okay, like guys, the heat is watching. Like I'm associated with you guys and it's gonna fuck up my geniality points. Like okay?

NEIL: Right on.

    (Pause.)

JACK: Hey, Neil?

NEIL: What?

JACK: I was wondering if you were gonna call up Cheryl when you get out.

NEIL: Cheryl? She's a cunt.

JACK: So you're not going to phone her?

NEIL: I don't phone cunts.

JACK: Then I guess you won't mind if I phone her?

NEIL: You phone her? What the fuck?

JACK: Hey, she always liked me, Neil. I just want you to know that I plan on calling her.

    (NEIL leaves.)

TONY: Fur of love. Fur of love.

Scene Eight
Tony's Confession

TONY: And the faggot was running ahead of us, but the other guys were faster 'cause, ah, 'cause they were faster. They got to the car before me. Then they were doing it, so I started doing it too. And when it was over, we just stood lookin', breathin' real hard. Later, when the cops let me go to the washroom, I went in there and saw spots of that man's blood on my face. That still really fucks me up. Sometimes I do this … *(Gesture of wiping blood off his face)* 'cause I'm still trying to get rid of the blood. I hate myself when I think that. It's kinda like why I wanna do some real good when I get out, you know, like clean the blood away and start fresh. Like Mr. Clean. A new life.

Scene Nine
Kisser

(The jail yard.)

JACK: Nineteen days and counting, you mothers.

BILLY: So what are we gonna do?

NEIL: You just play dumb, Billy-boy. They getta look at that cute little kisser of yours and they are gonna send you home to momma.

BILLY: I don't want to go home to momma.

NEIL: Why?

BILLY: 'Cause I'm too old for that.

NEIL: Billy-boy, you're just a little baby.

BILLY: Fuck off.

NEIL: Come to poppa.

BILLY: Fuck right off.

NEIL: What's the matter, man? Come on.

BILLY: Nothing. Everything keeps changing. That's all.

NEIL: Don't think about it.

JACK: Ya, Billy, you got that down look.

BILLY: I just hate waiting, okay?

TONY: Ya, me too. Too much to think about and like no way to plan.

JACK: Well, you gotta have a plan.

(JACK does pushups. TONY and BILLY join in. NEIL nonchalantly begins one arm pushups. The others watch. He does one. Tries to do two but falls. Jail buzzer.)

Scene Ten
Janitor

(Jail.)

JACK: It's a beautiful day. Whaddawe got?

BILLY: Ten days and counting.

JACK: I called her.

BILLY: What did you say?

JACK: None of your fucking business.

BILLY: Cool.

JACK: I gotta get some clothes before I see her. I look like a goddamn janitor. It's not me. Like I'm a handsome motherfucker.

NEIL: Ya, but Jack, Cheryl deserves a janitor.

JACK: And just what the fuck makes you the expert, all of a sudden, in what women want?

NEIL: My cock.

TONY: Wow, it talks.

JACK: *(To NEIL.)* You need help.

NEIL: No, I need out.

BILLY: And then what?

(Pause.)

TONY: Hey, a janitor, that would be good. The judge guy, he'd like that. You know, cleaning piss off things. I could do that. Ah, your honour, I want to be the kind of janitor who believes in the removal of dicks in order to make the washrooms more environ-mentally unfucked.

(They don't laugh. Buzzer.)

Scene Eleven
Jack's Confession

(Jail.)

JACK: I don't hate anybody. I mean, look, he shouldn't have died. It was strictly circumstantial. I wish he hadn't died. If one thing had been different that night, then the rest of it wouldn't have happened and I wouldn't be here. And I am here. But now it's time, time to move on. *(Pause.)* There's something I know I gotta do. *(Pause.)* I'm sorry. *(Pause.)* Fuck, that's hard.

Scene Twelve
Bachelor Pad

(Jail. NEIL is going for BILLY.)

NEIL: Don't say that. Don't fucking say that.

BILLY: Or what, Neil?

(NEIL grabs BILLY. JACK enters with TONY in tow.)

JACK: Three more mother-fucking days till Cheryl gets to like drool over the real thing. Cheryl, here I come.

(NEIL releases BILLY.)

BILLY: You hurt my fucking neck.

NEIL: I'm sorry, man.

BILLY: Well, don't do it.

NEIL: I won't. I won't. Jesus, you on the rag?

TONY: I am. Like I'm just freaked, man.

NEIL: Why?

TONY: Well, Franie said maybe she could put me up for a bit.

BILLY: Well, that's great.

TONY: Ya, but not right away.

BILLY: That's shit.

TONY: Ya. You?

BILLY: My mom.

NEIL: Suckers.

TONY: Fuck off, Neil.

JACK: Don't sweat it boys. Neil's got to stay with his horny old uncle.

NEIL: In the basement. My apartment. Bachelor fucking pad. So you can all go fuck yourselves.

BILLY: Well, I guess we'll have to.

(Buzzer.)

Scene Thirteen
Out

(Waiting for the hearings to begin, the guys speak their interior thoughts. These repeat until the OFFICIAL interrupts.)

NEIL: Nothing's over. I hate you. I'm scared.

TONY: I'm freaked. I'm pumped. Gonna lose it.

BILLY: Don't know. Wanna get drunk. I'm fucked.

JACK: Sorry. I've changed. I love you.

OFFICIAL: *(Voice-over.)* And what do you have to say for yourself?

(At the hearing.)

NEIL: I've done with the past and I want to look to the future to get established and to get my life together. My uncle is willing to apprentice me and I can live in his basement apartment until I get settled. I think that you should know that he goes to church. Sir, I believe I will find reintegration relatively smooth.

OFFICIAL: *(Voice-over.)* I'm concerned that your attitude is still aggressive.

JACK: Not at all, sir. If I may say so, I am quite used to the gay contingent in the prison.

OFFICIAL: *(Voice-over.)* Is that so?

BILLY: There will be no trouble from me. I just want to start fresh and do things right.

OFFICIAL: *(Voice-over.)* What did you learn in here?

TONY: I learned the difference between right and wrong.

OFFICIAL: *(Voice-over.)* You have a responsibility to remember what you learned.

NEIL: I know.

OFFICIAL: *(Voice-over.)* Pardon?

ALL: *(Together.)* I know, sir!

OFFICIAL: *(Voice-over.)* You are free to go.

(They explode with joy.)

Scene Fourteen
Babes

(The guys leave jail with suitcases. They gape at the world that roars by them. A woman shimmers in the distance.)

NEIL: Hey, babe!

JACK: Cheryl?

TONY: Franie!

BILLY: Mom?

(They all go their separate ways. BILLY waves to Contessa.)

Scene Fifteen
Never Too Fast

(Billy's mother's apartment. BILLY comes in.)

BILLY: Mom? … Mom? … You home? … Mom? … *(Looking around.)* Shit, she must be doing okay on her own.

(Phone rings. Finally, he answers.)

Hello?

(Light on JACK.)

JACK: Billy-boy.

BILLY: Jackman, yo.

JACK: What you doin', bro?

BILLY: Just standing here.

JACK: How's your mom?

BILLY: She's not here.

JACK: Sniffin' her undies?

BILLY: Dream on.

JACK: Shit, beep on the line. Call comin' in, man. Might be Cheryl.

BILLY: Really dream on, buddy.

JACK: Call you back.

(Hangs up. Light down on JACK. Phone rings.)

BILLY: *(Answering.)* That was fast.

(Light on TONY.)

TONY: Can never be too fast, man. Like you gotta be ready even for the cripples.

BILLY: Hey, man, what's up?

TONY: My dick. How's the place?

BILLY: Don't know.

TONY: Well, take a fucking look. You wouldn't believe the pukey colour they got in my room.

BILLY: Paint it then.

TONY: Jesus, man, I'm the guest.

BILLY: Look, Tony, I gotta go.

TONY: Okay.

BILLY: Later.

(BILLY hangs up. Light down on TONY. Phone rings. BILLY answers.)

I said, I gotta go.

(Light on NEIL.)

NEIL: Jesus, man. Is that how they taught you to talk to strangers?

BILLY: Neil?

NEIL: In the flesh.

BILLY: What's up?

NEIL: Taking stock, man.

BILLY: Ya, me too, but I don't know what to do now.

NEIL: Eat.

BILLY: I'm not hungry.

NEIL: Billy-boy, you just think you're not hungry. Stick your head in the fridge, okay?

BILLY: Then what?

NEIL: Then eat.

BILLY: Whatever, man. I gotta go.

(BILLY hangs up. Light down on NEIL. Billy's MOTHER enters.)

Mom! Holy shit! You look great.

(They hug.)

Scene Sixteen
New Love

(The street. JACK approaches CHERYL.)

JACK: Cheryl?

CHERYL: Hi, Jack.

JACK: Cheryl, shit. How are you?

CHERYL: Fine. How are you?

JACK: I'm fine. You?

CHERYL: I'm okay.

JACK: You look okay.

CHERYL: You look grown up.

JACK: Well, I've been working on it.

CHERYL: Oh ya?

JACK: Ya. I phoned you.

CHERYL: I know.

JACK: So, I saw you and thought, I don't know … I should come over and say hi, anyway.

CHERYL: Hi, anyway.

> *(They laugh.)*

JACK: You didn't phone back.

CHERYL: I hadn't made up my mind.

JACK: How come?

CHERYL: Don't know.

JACK: I don't have two heads.

CHERYL: Maybe it means I'm not interested in going out with you.

JACK: What makes you think I want to go out with you?

CHERYL: 'Cause I'm really fucking smart.

JACK: Oh?

CHERYL: Ya.

JACK: So how have you been?

CHERYL: Okay.

JACK: So what's new?

CHERYL: I'm just going to rent a movie. I've got to get home before five.

JACK: Seen *Titanic?*

CHERYL: Why?

JACK: 'Cause I'd like to see it with you.

> *(Pause.)*

CHERYL: So, you're back.

JACK: Ya, I'm back.

CHERYL: Was it scary in there?

JACK: Didn't you read my letters?

> *(Pause.)*

CHERYL: Got any plans?

JACK: My plan is to plan a plan.

CHERYL: I've got a kid, Jack. Now he wasn't planned.

JACK: How come I didn't know that? Wow. That's the wildest news I've had since I got out. You don't wear a ring.

CHERYL: Don't need to.

JACK: Ya?

CHERYL: Ya.

JACK: So show me your kid. I want to see if it's inbred or anything.

CHERYL: Shut up, you.

JACK: Or maybe he's just a dickin' head. A head in a bed. Just trying to get ahead in life.

> *(Laughing.)*

CHERYL: I've got to go. Call me.

JACK: No. You call me.

CHERYL: If you want to go out with me then phone me and we'll talk about it.

JACK: Why didn't you say that in the first place?

CHERYL: Bye.

> *(CHERYL leaves.)*

JACK: Okay, I'll call. I'll call you and, you know, tell you how much I like you, and how much you should like me. 'Cause no one should be alone, right?

Scene Seventeen
Muchachas

> *(Coffee shop. TONY is waiting. FRANIE comes in and sits.)*

FRANIE: Hey, little brother.

TONY: Franie, jesus, I'm so glad to see you.

FRANIE: I just had a feeling—I don't know—that you needed me or maybe I needed you, to know you're okay.

TONY: I'm trying to hang on, Franie.

FRANIE: I know. So give me a kiss already.

TONY: In front of everybody?

FRANIE: Yes, in front of everybody.

> *(They kiss.)*

TONY: Hey, I'm out, but like, I wanna come and stay with you guys. Mom and Dad are drivin' me nuts. Come on, just for a week or two. Just till I find another place.

FRANIE: No.

TONY: But you promised.

FRANIE: No.

TONY: Why don't you leave him?

FRANIE: Jesus, Tony.

TONY: Put your *muchachas* where your mouth is. Leave him.

FRANIE: I can't just leave him.

TONY: Well, that's how you leave.

FRANIE: He's dangerous.

TONY: So is breaking promises.

FRANIE: Don't even think about it.

TONY: What? I'm supposed to be scared of you. I'm a murderer, Franie.

> *(Pause.)*

FRANIE: Tony, calm down.

TONY: Why? Will it get me what I want?

FRANIE: It might.

TONY: Franie, I really need you now. Like you said.

FRANIE: So does my husband. I gotta go.

Scene Eighteen
Jello

> *(NEIL is in a bar. DOROTHY slides up.)*

DOROTHY: Hi.

NEIL: Hi.

DOROTHY: This seat taken?

NEIL: Ya … by you.

DOROTHY: Really? You new around here?

NEIL: Ya.

DOROTHY: You here alone?

NEIL: Waiting for a friend.

DOROTHY: I just dropped in after work. I like to unwind a bit. You?

NEIL: Me too.

DOROTHY: What are those dots?

NEIL: Tattoo.

DOROTHY: Oh.

NEIL: These are just fake. They wash off.

DOROTHY: How long you been out?

> *(Pause.)*

NEIL: Awhile.

DOROTHY: And you're available.

NEIL: Can I buy you a drink?

DOROTHY: Ya, but let's dance first.

(NEIL dances reluctantly.)

Am I torturing you?

NEIL: Hey, no. It's okay.

DOROTHY: So what did you do, kill someone or something?

NEIL: I don't talk about the joint.

DOROTHY: Come on, it makes you special.

NEIL: Bullshit.

DOROTHY: Well, special to me. I've never done it with a con before.

NEIL: What are you saying all this weird shit for?

DOROTHY: 'Cause I like you. You turn me on.

NEIL: What about those drinks?

DOROTHY: Let's go back to my place and get relaxed.

NEIL: I can't.

DOROTHY: How come?

NEIL: I'm meeting a friend, Tony.

DOROTHY: Ditch him.

NEIL: I can't. It's an old promise.

DOROTHY: Make a new promise?

NEIL: I can't.

DOROTHY: Then phone me.

NEIL: Absolutely.

(She writes her number on his hand.)

Hey, these numbers are fucked up.

DOROTHY: Gotta look in a mirror.

NEIL: Cool.

(She leaves. TONY comes in mimicking her dancing. They hug.)

Scene Nineteen
Billy's Mission

(The Contessa costume is nearby.)

BILLY: If you wanna change your life, you gotta change your life. That's what Contessa said, and she had *cajones*. I'm gettin' that now. I look at my mom and see what she did. Parents split up when I was in, but like she just turned it all around after that fucker left her. I can do that too. 'Cause what I figured out is that like this fear thing is what fucks people up. If I can get rid of the fear thing and get the old confidence back, well then everything will fall into place. Easy to say, right? *Cajones.* You gotta have *cajones* to be a fag. That's what it comes down to. Big mother-fucking *cajones.*

Scene Twenty
Curvy Legs

(Street. JACK is pacing. CHERYL hurries in.)

CHERYL: What? What happened?

JACK: Look, well, I'm glad you could come. Ah …

CHERYL: What?

JACK: I phoned so …

CHERYL: What do you want?

JACK: I phoned last night.

CHERYL: So?

JACK: And you didn't answer.

CHERYL: I wasn't there.

JACK: Ya, right. So I phoned you at work.

CHERYL: You interrupted me. My boss is waiting for me. You said it would take a second.

JACK: I didn't know. I just thought if you could come out for a minute … I wanted to see you again … now.

CHERYL: Because you have nothing better to do you think that you can screw me around with my boss.

JACK: No, no, no, this is going all wrong. All I was trying to do was say that I used to really like you, and like I like you now, and that we should therefore go out sometime.

CHERYL: Well, ya. That's not new news. Jesus, you're so impatient.

JACK: Look, I don't have money to go somewhere fancy. I just …

CHERYL: I don't care about money. Why don't you write me a love letter instead?

JACK: A love letter?

CHERYL: You do know what one of those are, don't you? You do know how to write. You did write to me after all.

JACK: Well, sure, but I never wrote one of those love letters before. Jesus.

CHERYL: Well maybe you'll learn.

JACK: What should I say?

CHERYL: Tell me all those things I won't let you do to me on Friday night.

JACK: Friday night?

CHERYL: Ya, come on over.

JACK: Really?

CHERYL: Ya, really.

JACK: Okay. *(He goes to kiss her and steps on her foot.)* I'm sorry.

CHERYL: It's okay, I got another one. Look, I gotta go.

JACK: Ya, sure. So write things like you're beautiful that kind of thing? Like you've got a great little nose, curvy legs …

CHERYL: Fast learner.

    (CHERYL leaves.)

JACK: Real fast.

Scene Twenty-one
Snake Hole

    (Coffee shop. TONY is waiting. FRANIE comes in and sits.)

FRANIE: Sorry. I'm late.

TONY: So give me a kiss already.

FRANIE: Fuck off.

TONY: You okay?

FRANIE: Ya, I just couldn't talk on the phone, 'cause he was right there.

TONY: May a snake go up his hole.

FRANIE: You're so gross.

TONY: Sorry.

FRANIE: Anyway, Frank started in on Carl 'cause he wouldn't stop crying. But I grabbed Carl away and locked us in the bathroom. And then the neighbour came so Frank had to settle down.

TONY: God bless neighbours. Carl okay?

FRANIE: Ya. He's at daycare. Tony, I gotta leave Frank.

TONY: Ya?

FRANIE: Ya.

Scene Twenty-two
Fuck a Duck

(Park: early evening. DOROTHY is putting on makeup.)

NEIL: So my uncle and me are driving along and this guy comes on the radio sayin' that on average an average human being lies about two hundred times a day. I said, who the hell has time to lie two hundred times a day? And Uncs says, every time you speak you can lie and not even know it. So I laugh and tell him to chew it, but said, you know, nicely. I don't want to piss him off or he'll give me a jolt of the two-twenty when I'm not looking, 'cause like he's an electrician. But about this lying shit, well all I've got to say is that it doesn't matter whether they are big lies or small lies. What really matters is if they are lies.

DOROTHY: I like you.

NEIL: Oh. I like you too.

DOROTHY: Thanks.

NEIL: Do you like it here?

DOROTHY: I guess.

NEIL: We could go on one of those boats, paddle around the pond.

DOROTHY: Ya, right.

NEIL: Or just sit here and neck. Ducks might get a hard-on.

DOROTHY: I thought we were going to go to a movie.

NEIL: Which one?

DOROTHY: You know, something sexy, but like not with guys heaving their dicks around like it was their brain or something.

NEIL: Christ, you're picky.

DOROTHY: Aren't you?

NEIL: I picked you.

DOROTHY: No you didn't. I picked you.

NEIL: Did not.

DOROTHY: Did too.

(NEIL tries to kiss her.)

My lipstick.

(They kiss. BILLY enters.)

NEIL: Fuck a duck! ... Billy-boy, what are you doing here?

BILLY: Free world. What happened to your mouth?

NEIL: Whaddaya think? *(Wipes his mouth.)* Is it gone?

BILLY: Sort of.

NEIL: Hey, great to see you man.

BILLY: Ya. Who's your friend?

NEIL: Dorothy this is Billy. Billy this is Dorothy.

> *(They shake hands.)*

DOROTHY: Nice tattoo.

BILLY: Thanks.

DOROTHY: I'm going to find a washroom. I'll be right back.

NEIL: You better be.

> *(DOROTHY leaves.)*

  Check out her body, man.

BILLY: First-class …

> *(Flashback to original murder. NEIL and BILLY are joined by JACK and TONY. JACK is lookout. The others are hiding.)*

BILLY: So we gonna do it or what?

JACK: Ya, man, ya … Fuck, here comes one.

NEIL: Don't get excited.

BILLY: Let's go smooth and quiet.

TONY: Like nothin's gonna happen.

JACK: Here he comes.

BILLY: We got a surprise for you, faggot.

NEIL: Shut up, Billy.

JACK: Come on, man. Let's get him.

TONY: He ain't going nowhere.

NEIL: Act like a faggot, man.

JACK: Here he comes. First blood, man. First fucking blood.

NEIL: This is gonna be better than an orgasm.

JACK: Fuckin' lay him out.

BILLY: Now!

> *(They rush the victim. JACK and TONY leave. Back to present.)*

NEIL: Hang for a few. We're just trying to decide what to do. Like a movie or something. Why don't you come?

BILLY: Three's a crowd.

NEIL: Come on, man.

BILLY: I mean, it would be great to hang with you, but parole and shit.

NEIL: New Van Damme, buddy.

BILLY: I can't. Call me.

> *(BILLY leaves.)*

NEIL: Shit!

> *(DOROTHY returns.)*

DOROTHY: Locked. Did he leave?

NEIL: Ya.

DOROTHY: He seems nice.

NEIL: He is. *(He kisses her.)* But not nearly as nice as you.

Scene Twenty-three
Tony's Mission

TONY: No doubt about this one. There's only one choice. It's simple: the law of survival. So what I have to do is take Frank, stake him to the ground and piss on him for a couple of days. Then I saw off his arms and legs so he has maximum trouble getting around, and ducktape his yap shut 'cause he's the kinda guy who likes to flap it. No one treats my sister like shit. I mean, if I didn't protect her what would I be worth? A bum crumb on the arse of life. You know, I can't believe that he would hit her. Hit a fucking woman, come on.

Scene Twenty-four
Smart Ass

> *(Night: outside Cheryl's place. JACK and CHERYL are finishing their date.)*

JACK: So? What?

CHERYL: Nothing.

JACK: You're bored. I can tell.

CHERYL: I am not.

JACK: Was it the Guido food?

CHERYL: Guido? Jack, my kid is half Italian. Do you mind?

JACK: Look, I didn't mean to insult your kid. I mean, with your influence I'm sure he can rise above his paternal gene stuff.

CHERYL: You are a dick.

JACK: No, I'm serious. Like people like to brand other people. You know, not give them a chance to show they've changed.

CHERYL: You've changed?

JACK: I have.

CHERYL: Still a smart ass.

JACK: But I'm a better smart ass.

CHERYL: Look, Jack, I've got a kid. I'm more cautious.

JACK: I don't have a kid and I'm more cautious too.

CHERYL: I've had a good time, really.

JACK: Like a really good time?

CHERYL: Ya. I had a really good time.

(JACK gets on his knees.)

JACK: So will you marry me?

(CHERYL disappears. Flash forward to the stag. BILLY, with the Contessa costume around him, points to a dead NEIL with JACK and TONY looking on in horror.)

Scene Twenty-five
The Kook

(Home of Billy's mother. MOTHER comes in. BILLY puts on scary music, sneaks up on her, and scares her.)

MOTHER: Billy, you can't do this anymore.

BILLY: I won't. I'm sorry. I just couldn't resist.

MOTHER: It's fine. I'm just used to living alone.

BILLY: Sure, Mom, sure.

MOTHER: Will you turn the music off?

BILLY: Oh, ya, ya.

(He turns the music off.)

Mom?

MOTHER: I'm late for work.

BILLY: Right … Mom, I'm sorry.

MOTHER: Billy, you've always been a kook. I've got to hurry.

BILLY: Sure.

MOTHER: I love you.

BILLY: Hard not to love a kook.

(MOTHER leaves.)

Mom, don't leave me, don't leave me.

Scene Twenty-six
Romeo

(Outside.)

JACK: How's Franie?

TONY: Cool. She's away from that fucker. If he comes around, I'll do him.

JACK: You?

TONY: Then we, you fucker.

JACK: We? Whaddaya mean we?

TONY: Come on, man. This is for Franie.

JACK: So?

TONY: So? I can't believe you're saying this to me. We're the brothers.

JACK: But we're not the stupid fucking brothers.

TONY: Here you go.

JACK: Listen to me, you dick. Listen to me.

TONY: No, you listen to me.

JACK: Tony, it's important.

TONY: I've got something important to say too.

JACK: Mine's more important.

TONY: Not fucking possible.

JACK: Wanna bet?

TONY: Don't be a goober. Just listen to me.

JACK: You listen to me.

TONY: Jack …

JACK: Tony, I'm going to get married.

(Pause.)

TONY: To what?

JACK: To Cheryl.

TONY: Chew me.

JACK: I'm serious.

TONY: Holy fuck. You're serious.

JACK: Serious about marrying.

TONY: Jesus, Jack, you're pretty young to be going down the drain. When?

JACK: Don't worry. You're not invited.

TONY: What does she see in you anyway?

JACK: More'n you'll ever know.

TONY: So, you then like like her?

JACK: She's got something special, man.

TONY: Tits.

JACK: No. You're missing the point.

TONY: Two points.

JACK: No, man. I just keep thinking about her all the time.

TONY: Like doing her? That kind of stuff.

JACK: No. Like ya, but no.

(BILLY enters, walking slowly towards the Contessa costume, but speaks as if he is with JACK and TONY)

TONY: Hey, Billy-boy.

BILLY: Brothers.

JACK: You're lookin' good, man.

TONY: Guess what?

BILLY: What?

JACK: Let me tell him.

BILLY: What?

TONY: He's gonna be getting it wet regular now.

(JACK and TONY get lost in their fun. Flashback to prison. NEIL enters.)

NEIL: Don't you say that! Don't you fucking say that!

BILLY: Or what, Neil?

(NEIL rips down the costume and leaves with it. Back to present. BILLY turns and continues, slowly proceeding out. As before, he speaks as if he is with JACK and TONY.)

JACK: I asked Cheryl to marry me, Billy-boy.

TONY: Can you believe that shit?

BILLY: That's fucking fantastic. You're not shitting me?

JACK: For sure and for real.

BILLY: Fuck me. That's great. When?

TONY: Don't worry. You're not invited.

JACK: Soon, Billy-boy. Soon.

BILLY: That's gonna be some party.

(BILLY is finally gone, but then returns, joining JACK and TONY during the following speech.)

JACK: I've got this beautiful picture of her in my head. She's got nothing on. She smiles at me and I run my hand down between her breasts. I take one in my mouth. Her nipple is hard. I bite. She moans … I love this part … My hand slides onto her thigh and between her legs and she is drooling love all over me. My mouth dives into hers, and it's like I become her, and feeling this feeling, right, that rises in me and I know is in her … Man, if this isn't perfection, I don't know what is.

TONY: Now you're talkin'!

BILLY: Fuck me. We should party now.

TONY: Now?

BILLY: Ya. The guy's gotta have a stag.

JACK: A guy doesn't get married every day.

Scene Twenty-seven
Coming

> *(Intermingled with NEIL and DOROTHY fucking on a couch is BILLY's monologue.)*

NEIL: Oh fuck. Oh jesus.

BILLY: In the dark, in the shadow, I touch someone.

NEIL: It's coming. It's coming.

BILLY: I walk into the arms that squeeze me hard.

NEIL: Come on. Come on. Jesus, coming, coming, ah, ah.

BILLY: We press against each other.

DOROTHY: Neil! Neil!

BILLY: I open my mouth and kiss him.

NEIL: I'm gonna. It's coming.

BILLY: He pulls me down, his hands under me, taking me.

DOROTHY: It's not working.

NEIL: Come on, come on, jesus, coming, coming, ah, ah.

BILLY: There's nothing else in the world but the two of us.

DOROTHY: Neil, lighten up.

BILLY: All I know is how I feel and I don't want it to change, ever. His eyes are like black diamonds on this night. I loved him, but he didn't love me. And that's the way it is.

> *(BILLY disappears. NEIL falls off the couch.)*

NEIL: Christ, what are you doing?

DOROTHY: Are you all right?

NEIL: Course I'm all right.

DOROTHY: Don't worry about it.

NEIL: Worry about what?

    (NEIL tries to come on to her.)

DOROTHY: Fuck off!

    (She leaves.)

Scene Twenty-eight
Rounds

    (TONY is waiting impatiently. FRANIE enters.)

TONY: Where have you been?

FRANIE: Fucked up day.

TONY: Then I'm gonna fuck it up even more with this news.

FRANIE: Jesus, what?

TONY: They phoned from the daycare.

FRANIE: Jesus. What's the matter?

TONY: Frank tried to take Carl from there.

FRANIE: This is all fucked up.

    (Shift to JACK and CHERYL.)

JACK: I adore you.

CHERYL: Prove it.

JACK: I do. All the time.

CHERYL: You have to prove it every day. Until I'm dead.

JACK: Nice!

    (Shift to BILLY and his MOTHER.)

BILLY: Mom, there was this guy … in prison.

MOTHER: It's okay.

BILLY: You don't even know what I'm gonna say.

MOTHER: It's still okay. I love you.

    (She leaves.)

BILLY: Would you still love me if I was a fag?

Scene Twenty-nine
Neil's Mission

(NEIL on the phone.)

NEIL: Hi, Dorothy, it's Neil. Pick up the phone. Please. I really need to talk to you.

(NEIL hangs up. He puts on music and does a punching routine.)

See, you gotta have your act together. No time for hesitation. Get set up, figure out the moves and things go right every time. Next time I see Dorothy, it's gonna go gangbusters. Like Dorothy is cool, weird cool, but definitely heavy on the cool and just a little on the weird. Maybe like me, right? So when we get down to, you know, doing it next time, well I'm fuckin' gonna blow my cum to the moon and she's gonna cream like the Apollo mission.

(NEIL leaves. Phone rings. Voice-over.)

DOROTHY: Neil, it's me. I'm here. I just missed you. Why don't you come over tonight if you're not doing anything. I mean, we could look at the stars, or whatever.

(She hangs up.)

Scene Thirty
The Stag, part "A"

(Night: Neil's apartment. The guys enter, beers in hand. They move to the throbbing music. They become the four brothers, who once again ride into the sunset.

Scene Thirty-one
The Stag, part "B"

(Later. Drinking.)

NEIL: Little present for you later on, Jack-man. You'll be lickin' your bag and your chops for the rest of the week.

JACK: You fuckers. What's going on?

NEIL: Nothin'. Tony?

TONY: Nothin'. Billy?

BILLY: Nothin', man. Absolutely nothin's goin' on.

JACK: Fuck you guys.

Scene Thirty-two
The Stag, part "C"

(Later. Drinking.)

BILLY: Who's your best man?

JACK: Don't know.

TONY: How many ushers?

JACK: Don't know ... Okay, where is she?

BILLY: Who?

JACK: Come on.

BILLY: Concentrate. You gotta get a best man.

NEIL: You gotta get a bridesmaid. Right here on the floor.

JACK: Okay, who is she?

TONY: Jeez, Jack, you don't even know who the bridesmaid is?

JACK: No, man, I'm talking about ...

BILLY: Like you should pick someone, not us, so there's no, you know, competition.

NEIL: Pick me.

BILLY: Actually, I think I'd be better.

JACK: I wouldn't pick any of you saps.

BILLY: You should do it in a church.

NEIL: Get serious.

BILLY: Like I am serious. I know there isn't like a fucking god, but if for some reason there is, then you're just hedging your bets.

TONY: Ya, Jack, you gotta be responsible now.

JACK: Lick bag.

Scene Thirty-three
The Stag, part "D"

(Later. Drinking.)

JACK: Hey, Billy-boy, you're lookin' down. You're not drinking?

BILLY: I'm drinking.

JACK: Then not enough. Don't worry. Wacky Jackie is still gonna be around. No broad is gonna tame me.

TONY: *(To NEIL.)* He'll be lickin' her ass forever.

NEIL: Fuckin' tragedy.

BILLY: It's just sad, man.

JACK: Billy-boy. I'm still me. I'll still be me when I'm getting it legal. Come on. We're friends forever.

NEIL: Till death do us part.

TONY: Friends forever.

BILLY: You mean it?

JACK: To the brothers. Chugfest!

JACK, TONY and NEIL: *(Together.)* One, two, three, four, five, six, seven, eight, nine, ten!

> *(BILLY chugs beer.)*

JACK: It's my party and you're my friends. Always were, always will be, for ever and ever. Abooze.

ALL: *(Together.)* Party! Party! Party!

JACK: Where's my surprise?

NEIL, TONY and BILLY: *(Together.)* Party! Party! Party!

> *(JACK and TONY do a bumfuck grunt and then fall apart laughing.)*

Scene Thirty-four
The Stag, part "E"

(Later. Drinking.)

NEIL: I remember when we had everything. The world was just laid out before us. It was always gonna be a wild stag that would never end.

JACK and TONY: *(Together.)* Yes, sir!

NEIL: But what are we left with? Just bullshit. Bullshit, bullshit, bullshit.

BILLY: Right on.

NEIL: No one tells me I can't drink. No one!

BILLY: Fuckin' A!

Scene Thirty-five
The Stag, part "F"

(Later. Drinking.)

TONY: So Franie and I …

NEIL: *(Mimicking.)* "Franie and I …"

TONY: … get little Carl home …

NEIL: "… get little Carl home …"

TONY: ... to the apartment and Frank, who tried to grab the kid at daycare, comes pounding on the door, drunk as a skunk.

NEIL: Bullshit.

JACK: No shit.

TONY: Well, there was actually a lot of shit. Like I was holding the dirty diaper that Franie had just given me. I opened the door and handed it to him and like slammed the door. He's such a fuckin' goof. So then I phoned the super, the neo-Nazi with the walking jaw-dog or something, and I told him there was a faggot wiping shit on the walls. So the super lets Jaws go to work on Frank, and you know what, that son of a bitch won't be back.

BILLY: Jeez, Neil, looks like Tony stole your balls right out from under your hood.

NEIL: Still got enough to punch your lights out, man.

BILLY: Oooo, I'm scared. Oooo.

TONY: Ya, we're scared.

JACK: Freakin', man. I'm freakin'. I'm freakin'.

NEIL: You guys are too much.

Scene Thirty-six
The Stag, part "G"

(Later. BILLY is not there. NEIL is holding JACK upright. TONY comes in with a cardboard box that is decorated as a vagina. They are more drunk.)

TONY: Well man, we got a few things together to send you on your merry way.

JACK: I love you fucking guys.

NEIL: And you're gonna love us more when you get your pud in the noose.

JACK: Tony, Neil, Billy-boy, I love you. Billy? Billy?

NEIL: He's busy.

TONY: And I put my hand in her box and I pull out fancy lacy panties.

(They put them on JACK's head.)

And to go with that, I put my hand into her box and I pull out ... edible underwear.

NEIL: Just in case her cooking ain't up to scratch.

TONY: Even if it is, like these would be good at a dinner party or something. Good conversational piece.

JACK: I'll eat them and think of you.

TONY: Oh, wow. I'm hard.

>   *(NEIL takes the box.)*

NEIL: And I put my hand in her box and I pull out ... a can of beans.

JACK: I love beans.

NEIL: This is for safety reasons man. Just in case you gotta slow her down 'cause like you can't handle it. Like wolf the can cold. Then begin foreplay under the covers.

JACK: I like that part.

NEIL: Then do the S.B.D., brother—the "silent but deadly." She'll be out for a week. Like you can come and visit us.

JACK: Her toes are beautiful, man. I like to suck them.

TONY: Fuck, man, that's gross.

JACK: Is not. I love them.

TONY: Christ. You really need help, Jack. And so I put my hand in her box and I pull out ... a fly swatter.

JACK: You guys are the greatest.

TONY: We know, Jack, that you basically stink, you know, like fucking B.O. like a dead antelope, so this little baby is for the broad, so when you're banging her she can swat the flies off your ass so you're like not distracted.

JACK: I love you guys.

NEIL: Ya, Jack.

JACK: Like not like, but like love.

NEIL: Ya, Jack.

JACK: And I'm gonna miss you guys.

TONY: Well, I'm reaching into her box for one more goody from the boys ... a videotape.

JACK: I love tapes.

TONY: Well, you'll really love this one, 'cause it's one of you beatin' your meat.

JACK: What the fuck?

TONY: Look at the title. "Jack Beating Off."

JACK: What the fuck?

NEIL: Tony taped you when you were in the can.

JACK: What the fucking fuck?

TONY: You moan real cute, Jack.

JACK: Let me see that.

> *(He throws it to NEIL. JACK tries to get it. NEIL throws it to TONY. More throwing.)*

Scene Thirty-seven
The Stag, part "H"

JACK: You guys don't know about love until you meet a Cheryl.

> *(TONY sits JACK down.)*

NEIL: *(As M.C.)* Okay, okay. Hello, there, motherfucks. It's a cool evening in the big city and there are a million stories to be told, but the really big "shew" in town is a lovely little lady …

JACK: Oh, man, I knew it.

NEIL: … who has a perfect set of hoolas …

TONY: Yes!

NEIL: … and an ass that deserves your sass.

JACK: You shouldn't have.

NEIL: All right, all right. Ladies and gentlemen, let's hear it for … What do I call her, man?

TONY: Who knows.

NEIL: Let's hear it for …

> *(Music. BILLY enters in drag. He is wearing Contessa's costume.)*

BILLY: Here's to a new life, Jack.

> *(BILLY does his walking routine for the boys. They cheer him on. BILLY makes JACK dance. NEIL breaks in and grabs BILLY roughly, grinding in to him.)*

JACK: Easy does it, man.

NEIL: Fuck off.

BILLY: Stop it.

TONY: You're hurting him, man.

NEIL: Fuck you.

> *(BILLY and NEIL fight, rolling on the floor.)*

TONY: I don't mind saying that you two look like a couple of *faggots!!*

NEIL: *(To TONY.)* Get away from me, you fuck!

JACK: Back off, Tony.

> *(BILLY pins NEIL.)*

BILLY: Faggot!

NEIL: Stop it, Billy.

BILLY: Faggot needs a kiss.

(BILLY kisses NEIL. NEIL accepts. JACK and TONY chant.)

JACK and TONY: *(Together.)* Uga chugga uga chugga ...

(BILLY breaks the kiss. He stands and grabs a beer.)

BILLY: I'd like to make a toast to Neil. The best fuck I've ever had. *(BILLY drinks.)* Again. *(Drinks.)* And again. *(Drinks.)* And again. *(Drinks.)* And again.

(NEIL tries to shut BILLY up. BILLY knees him. NEIL falls. BILLY kicks him and keeps kicking him until he is dead. JACK and TONY finally drag BILLY away from NEIL.)

Scene Thirty-eight
Contessa

(BILLY wears Contessa's costume.)

BILLY: Contessa was the range drag queen. He was pretty sick then but still liked to dress up. Just stayed in his cage. People would go and visit him. I didn't know him, so I never went there at the beginning, right? But one day this guy tells me the queen is asking for me. I'm saying what the fuck. I don't want to talk to no drag queen. But like everybody talked to him, right, so if I didn't I'd draw heat. They all knew something was up, 'cause when I walked down the range to the queen, everybody started moving in behind me and like making fun of me. But I just go right on. I'm committed to this thing 'cause I know I'm caught. So I come up to his drum and look in and there he is, Contessa in blue sequins right up his AIDS fucking death look, and a huge red mouth and holes for eyes and the bleach blond mountain of hair shit on his head. But he's lying in his bed 'cause he can't stand. He's too weak. Everyone is listening. In this cracked voice he says to me, "I hear you did in one of my faggot brothers. You gonna do me too? That what you want to do? Why don't you come and visit me tomorrow? I don't bite. Spike's got some new leather porn you can read to me. Will you do that, fag killer?"

(The end.)